THAT'S OUR CUSTODIAN!

The author and photographer would like to thank all the many teachers, administrators, other faculty members, children, and parents at P.S. 87, Manhattan, for their inspiring school and generous cooperation in the making of this book. Special thanks to Stephen Brown for all his wonderful help and support in the preparation of the manuscript.

Library of Congress Cataloging-in-Publication Data
Morris, Ann, 1930-
That's our custodian!/Ann Morris; photographs and illustrations by Peter Linenthal.
p. cm.—(That's our school)
Summary: Introduces Earl Carroll, an elementary school custodian, describing what he does during the school day and how he interacts with other staff and students.
ISBN 0-7613-2401-1 (lib. bdg.)
1. School custodians—Juvenile literature.   [1. School custodians.   2. Occupations.]   I. Linenthal, Peter, ill.
II. Title.   III. Series: Morris, Ann, 1930-   . That's our school.
LB3235.M67   2003
371.6'8—dc21   2002155133

The Millbrook Press, Inc.
2 Old New Milford Road
Brookfield, Connecticut 06804
www.millbrookpress.com

THAT'S OUR CUSTODIAN!

Ann Morris

Photographs and Illustrations
by Peter Linenthal

The Millbrook Press / Brookfield, Connecticut

Earl Carroll is the custodian in our
school, and we think he's terrific!
He's also a friend, a teacher, a storyteller, and a singer.
We call our custodian Speedo—the name that was
given to him when he was a member of a famous
singing group, The Cadillacs.
All his good friends call him Speedo, and because
we're his good friends, we call him Speedo, too.
Sometimes Speedo sings a song
that goes like this: "They often call me
Speedo, but my real name is Mr. Earl."

Our custodian's job is keeping our
school clean and in good repair.
Speedo is very proud of our building
and works hard to take care of it.
Each morning when Speedo comes
to work he checks in on a special machine.
This machine keeps track of how many hours he works.
Then Speedo begins his job.
First he goes up and down the stairs dusting and
sweeping, cleaning the windows along the way.
Next he goes from room to room,
checking to make sure that they are clean.

Our custodian is in charge of all the rooms
in the building—the classrooms, the halls,
the offices, the auditorium, the gymnasium,
the lunchroom, and the bathrooms.
He sweeps and mops all these rooms.
He cleans all the lights, the windows,
and the doorways.
He cleans the sinks and the toilets.
He often sings as he works.

Sometimes we help him
sweep up all the mess
that we make when
we do our projects. He
says we're good helpers!

Terrific!

Our lunchroom gets really messy. When we have finished eating, our custodian throws away any papers or bottles that we have left around. Then he washes the floor and wipes off the tables.

He often stops by our table to say hello.
He teaches us songs and tells us funny stories.
He makes us laugh. We like it when Speedo
visits us in the lunchroom.

As our custodian cleans the building, he makes sure the bathrooms have fresh paper towels, toilet paper, and soap. If new supplies are needed, he makes sure they are sent to our school. He also checks to make sure that everything in the building is in good repair. If things are broken, he either fixes the problem himself or calls a person who knows how to do the repair job.

Our custodian also helps with special events like graduation, school plays, and assemblies. When we plan an assembly, he meets with our teachers to see if we need anything special on the stage or extra seats in the auditorium. He checks to make sure the curtains are working, and that everything is safe and clean. He's always willing to help in whatever way he can.

At the end of each day our custodian collects the trash, puts new plastic bags in all the wastebaskets, and empties the garbage into large black bags.

Then he puts the bags outside where a garbage truck picks them up. "It is important to collect the trash every day," he says, because food and garbage bring mice into the building. Trash will also decay and make a place where germs can grow, and these germs can make you very sick.

Speedo makes friends with all of us. "How are my kids?" he asks when he sees us. Sometimes he shows us magic tricks. He's like a big dad to many of us. He gives us hugs and "high fives"—but when he does, he wants us to do pushups. We think that's funny. We really like having Speedo around.

Our teachers like him, too.

Our custodian works very hard, and by the end of the day he is pretty tired. Sometimes after school he buys an ice-cream cone from the ice-cream man near our school.

We like ice cream, too!

This is the public school in Harlem that Speedo went to when he was a little boy.

Speedo loved the singer Bojangles.

Speedo grew up and went to school in Harlem, a part of New York City. He always loved to sing, and when he was about ten or eleven, he entered a talent contest at his school.

Speedo and his friends window-shop in Harlem.

He sang "Sweet Georgia Brown," a song one of his favorite singers, Bill "Bojangles" Robinson, used to sing. When he was sixteen, he joined a group of boys who met together on street corners to sing—this was called "street corner singing."

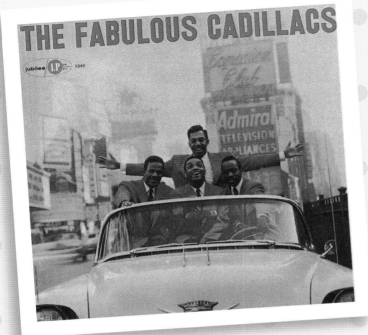

Then . . .   **. . . and now**

Later, Speedo joined The Cadillacs and traveled all over the country with them. He loved singing with the group, but he remembers there were hard times, too. In those days it was hard for black people to find a room to stay in. The Cadillacs became very famous singing a kind of music called doo-wop, and they made many recordings.

The Cadillacs are still good friends. Sometimes they visit the famous Apollo Theatre in Harlem where they used to perform.

Sometimes Speedo brings some of The Cadillacs to our school to sing for us.

We're so lucky to have Speedo in our school. **THAT'S OUR CUSTODIAN!**

THINGS TO DO

Would you like to know more about your custodian or what it is like to be a custodian?

Would you like to do something nice for your custodian?

Try one of these activities.

Learn About Your Custodian

- Follow your custodian around the school for a morning and ask him or her about all the things he or she is doing.

- Take some photographs of your custodian at work.

- Ask your custodian to tell you what school was like when he or she was your age.

Make a Poster

- Make a poster about your custodian with pictures you have drawn or photographs you have taken. Give it to your custodian to put up.

Have Fun with Your Custodian

- Ask your custodian to join your class in a ballgame or picnic.

- Make a tape of some of the songs, jokes, or stories that you and your custodian share.

About the Author

Ann Morris loves children, and she loves writing books
for children. She has written more than eighty books for
children, including a series of books for The Millbrook
Press about grandmothers and their grandchildren called
What Was It Like, Grandma? For many years Ann Morris
taught school. Eventually, she left teaching to become
an editor with a children's book publishing company.
While she still sometimes teaches workshops and
seminars for teachers, Ann Morris now spends most
of her time writing. She lives in New York City.

About the Photographer-Illustrator

Peter Linenthal is a talented photographer and illustrator.
He studied fine arts at the San Francisco Art Institute.
He is a native of California and teaches at the San Francisco
Center for the Book. Peter Linenthal also loves children
and working on books for children. He did the photographs
and illustrations for Ann Morris's books about grandmothers.